Homeground

Drama Series 5

Caterina Edwards

Homeground

A Play

Guernica

Montreal, 1990

For Pietro and Ausilia
who made this land their home.

Copyright © 1990 by Guernica Editions
and Caterina Edwards.
All rights reserved.
Printed in Canada.

Antonio D'Alfonso
Guernica Editions Inc.
P.O. Box 633, Station N.D.G.
Montréal (Québec), Canada H4A 3R1

The Publisher acknowledges financial
support from The Canada Council.

Canadian Cataloguing in Publication Data
Edwards, Caterina, 1948-
Homeground
(Drama series ; 5)
ISBN 0-920717-02-0
I. Title. II Series.
PS8559.D83H64 1989 C812'.54 C88-090066-0
PR9199.3.E39H64 1989

The Characters
Maria: Late twenties and lovely, in a simple way.
Cesare: Her husband; late thirties, thin and intense.
Candida: early twenties, cute; recently married to Nico, who used to board in Maria and Cesare's house.

The Boarders
Lucio: Late twenties and handsome.
Mario: Early twenties but acts as if he were seventeen.
Riccardo: Thirty and self confident.

The Children
Beppino: five.
Mimma: The baby... a bundle or a doll.
A Postman: Since the postman wears a cap, he can be played by the actor who portrays Mario.
Seven actors are needed.

Homeground was premiered, under the title *Tierra straniera,* in a somewhat different form in August, 1986 at the Edmonton Fringe Festival. Directed by Lynn Fredine, produced by Geoffrey Jackson and with set by Brock Lumsden, the cast was as follows:

Maria	Irene Blum
Cesare	Lenny Greenwood
Candida	Donna Fraser
Lucio	John Rusich
Riccardo	Perry Harris
Mario and Postman	Maxwell T. Wilson
Beppino	Michael Leskow

Fall, 1961.

A large kitchen-dining-living room takes up most of the stage. A short hallway and stairs lead up to a second level where a landing and a cluttered room are visible. The furniture is shabby. The large area should include a table, a rocking chair and a cradle. There are two doors, one by the kitchen and one by the hallway stairs.

The prologue, Maria's monologue, the dialogue between Lucio and Cesare, and the epilogue should be marked off in some stylised way from the naturalistic parts of the play, possibly through lighting or through the use of one area of the stage.

SCENE 1

A few bars of the music to "Terra straniera" as the lights come up. Cesare is buttoning up his shirt; Maria is putting Cesare's lunch in his lunchbox. As they speak, Maria brings him his boots and the rest of his winter gear. She helps him put on his coat and scarf in a ritualistic manner.

CESARE

For years I worked at two jobs. On construction from seven till one, six days a week. And as a janitor, three till eleven, for five days. Work, work and more work.

MARIA

I was so tired that I had almost forgotten how to think. Washing and ironing, cooking and dishes for all the men. Sewing, scrubbing floors and walls, and the little ones, always.

CESARE

Whenever my arms ached...

MARIA

Whenever I thought I could not move one more step...

CESARE

I would start to count up how much money I was making: $1.25 an hour, fourteen hours a day. Then... then, I could move, faster and faster. I could fly.

MARIA

Listening to him, I could see the money we were saving — not just as numbers in a bank book — but as ever growing piles of gold coins.

CESARE

The more gold, the more bricks, the sooner we would have a house and land of our own. We would be home, home at last.

MARIA

No more ice, no more snow. No more six- month winters. No more emptiness. Home, home at last.

CESARE

I chose the perfect spot for our house before I left. With a view of our flower-filled valley.

MARIA

And within view of my father's farm, my sister's house. Home.

CESARE

At last.

After a formal kiss, Cesare leaves by the side door.

MARIA

Home.

She turns to the cradle.

Little one.

SCENE II

A Saturday afternoon in November.

Maria is sitting in the rocking chair, babe in arms. As she speaks, Lucio enters by the front door, carrying a rifle. He creeps upstairs. A small light remains on him while he is in his room.

MARIA

She sings.

" *Terra straniera*
Quanta malinconia... "
(Foreign land
So much melancholy...)
No, no. Don't stare at me. Close those eyes... Close. Why don't you ever sleep when your brother does? Your Mamma has so much to do. Yes, little girl. A woman's life. Did you eat enough? Are you hungry? You must sleep... oh, sleep means nothing to you now but, believe me, one day, one day, it will. You will regret every hour when you could have slept and didn't. Come on, Mimma, close. I know it's nice, rocking like this. Rocking. Safe, in your Mamma's arms. Safe. Ah...

" *Io penso alla notte ed alla mia casetta*
Alla mia vecchietta che sempre aspetta,
Mamma, moriró di nostalgia
L'amore del paese e della Mamma
E' un gran fiamma ché bruscia mio cuore. "

(I think of night and my little house
Of my mother who always awaits
Mamma, I will die of nostalgia.

The love of one's country and of one's mother
Is a great flame that burns in my heart.)

> *She carries the baby over to the cradle.*
> *When she turns, she catches sight of Lucio*
> *who has entered the room and has been*
> *listening to her. He is carrying a shirt.*

MARIA

Lucio.

LUCIO

My shirt. I ripped the sleeve this morning. Do you
think it is fixable?

MARIA

Here? Of course. Two minutes work.

LUCIO

I have never heard you sing before.

MARIA

You have. Can you pass me my basket? How many
evenings have we sat, singing, around this table?
Thank you. I do not just move my lips.

LUCIO

But not alone. I have never heard you sing alone.
Your voice so clear... And that song. When I left
home, in the station of Citadella...

MARIA

I know, the whole group of you standing on the
platform, waiting for the train...

LUCIO

My mother and Milvia crying, me searching for
something to say...

MARIA

Gigietto Moro began to sing. Cesare has told me many times.

LUCIO

No, someone else began. Someone's brother. He was laughing, turning it into a joke. Then Gigietto joined in and his voice was so strong that he drowned him out.

MARIA

And gradually you all began to sing, the relatives, friends, the fiancées, everyone.

LUCIO

No, only Moro. The rest of us stood and listened. We had no idea then what it would be like. Listening to that song, we began to guess.

MARIA

Moro dead, not three months later in Whitehorse. *Che destino.*

LUCIO

Fate.

MARIA

There, done. I don't care what that coroner said. It was this country.

Lucio

He said that it was fate. Inevitable. And Gigetto knew, that day on the platform. You could hear it in his voice. Death was waiting for him, her arms wide.

MARIA

To die so far from home.

LUCIO

Sing it again. Or sing another song. Sing for me.

MARIA

Coffee?

LUCIO

No.

MARIA

You haven't had lunch. I could warm up some soup.

LUCIO

"*Terra straniera.*" One time, all the way through. Please. *Italia mia.*

MARIA

You haven't been eating. Not the way you should be. I know...

LUCIO

Sing, for me.

MARIA

Please, do not insist.

LUCIO

It was like a dream. So clear. When you stopped... Sing. I need to hear you.

MARIA

I have to get these dishes done.

LUCIO

Come on. Wash and sing if you must. For me.

MARIA

Did you shoot anything?

LUCIO

Shoot?

MARIA

Didn't you go hunting? I saw you early this morning, heading for the shed. Just after the other men left. I thought maybe you caught up with them.

LUCIO

I did not go hunting.

MARIA

But you went to the shed.

Maria begins to wash the dishes.

LUCIO

Target shooting. Bottles. Cans. Cans of soup are the best. I have a special place. No one else knows. I carry the stuff out with me. It is a little far, but it is worth the drive. When I have all the cans lined up on the fence, I stand way back.

Lucio is acting out his words.

I aim, my eye sharp, my hand steady, so steady, the rifle is part of me. Then, bam, bam, bam, so quickly. I barely have time to enjoy the targets being blasted away, spraying. I am good, very good. You should see me. I have always been good. That is why I do not understand. I was aiming for his leg. I was.

MARIA

The thief?

LUCIO

I told you? You know? I did not want anyone to know. I left it behind me, I left all the whispers, all those looks back there.

MARIA

Calm yourself, Lucio. You told me years ago. I never mentioned it to anyone. I don't gossip.

LUCIO

When? When did I tell you? It is Cesare. He found
out. He has to know everything. He has to control...

MARIA

No, it was you who told me. Remember, when I first
arrived.

*She is trying to cajole him into a calmer
mood.*

I was a new bride. I hardly knew Cesare. I was in this
strange place, with all these young men. You talked
to me. Cesare was working all the time. I didn't
know how to cook and everyone was flabbergasted.

She imitates different voices.

"What about all the feasts we dreamt of?" — "I
thought all good country girls could cook." —
"Another dream down the toilet." — And to Cesare:
"You should have given her a test before commit-
ting yourself." You didn't tease; you gave me those
cooking lessons. And you would talk...

LUCIO

When I came, I left it there, all of it.

MARIA

You do need a coffee.

LUCIO

It was a mistake. Do not listen to any of them. It was
a mistake. I did not intend...

MARIA

Of course it was.

LUCIO

A new life. I thought it was possible.

MARIA

Of course. New country, new...

LUCIO

I thought.

MARIA

How is the job hunting going?

> *She places a plate of cookies out on the table for him.*

LUCIO

Job?

MARIA

Nico said the cement plant in St. Albert might be looking for men.

LUCIO

Cement plant? With my lungs? My mother would turn over in her grave.

MARIA

Have you tried the meat packing plant? Riccardo said —

> *She puts down a cup of coffee for him.*

LUCIO

Why all the harping about work? You know I have not been feeling well.

> *He sits at the table and takes a hasty sip of coffee.*

> *Maria pushes the cookies closer to him.*

MARIA

Don't be offended. Come on — try the *Sospiri*. Made yesterday. I think you would be happier if you were working again. You have not been quite your-self since you got laid off...

LUCIO

There are no jobs, no decent jobs. I was not brought up for brute labour. I am tired of it, tired of being reduced to a beast of burden. No more.

MARIA

That is the way it is for all of us here. At least, at first. If you don't work, if you don't sweat, there is no chance of buying your way out.

She takes a dish towel off a large bowl that is on the side, pokes her finger into the bowl and then carries the bowl and a sack of flour to the table.

LUCIO

Okay. Okay. Tell the truth for once. You are after the rent money.

MARIA

How can you say that? Have I asked? Even once? Has Cesare? It has been five months; others would have asked, insisted.

LUCIO

You care about me?

MARIA

Why wouldn't I?

Pause.

When Beppino was born, those first months of his screaming hour after hour. I couldn't have stood it without your help.

Again, she pokes the dough.

LUCIO

I used to rub his back. That sometimes helped. Or I sang to him, the songs my mother used to sing to me.

16

MARIA

I would have gone crazy. Alone in the house, the cold pushing in. Once I gave him to you the moment you walked in. You looked at my face and whisked him off for a car ride. Oh, I don't forget.

Lucio rises and approaches Maria.

Why are you looking at me that way?

Maria has edged around the table so they are facing each other.

LUCIO

Let me touch you.

MARIA

No, don't...

She crosses her arms over her breast, as if to protect herself.

LUCIO

I need to touch you. I have been thinking and waiting so long. I know you have been too.

MARIA

Me? No.

LUCIO

I have felt you calling me.

MARIA

Keep away.

LUCIO

You need me as much as I need you. You need a man who knows how to love a woman.

MARIA

Cesare is the only one I need.

LUCIO

Him. Ha, I have heard him boast that you are the
only woman he has made love to. Cesare...? Don't
make me laugh.

MARIA

No. You are the ridiculous one.

LUCIO

You just do not know what it would be like. I know
how to love you. I could take you to the stars.

MARIA

The stars? That's an old one.

LUCIO

I could. Give me your hand. Maria, please. I won't
grab you. Just your hand.

MARIA

I have no time for this.

LUCIO

I remember too, you know, all the stories you told
me about your father and your house, about how
you would fight with the twins, grand battles with
slingshots and olives, and how you stole your
sister's lipstick. You had a favourite circle of pine
trees, a special field of wildflowers.

MARIA

The bread.

She sprinkles flour.

It is time to knead the bread.

Lucio has managed to move a bit closer.

LUCIO

You could go back, recapture it all, in my arms...
The caress of a petal, the brightness of the stars.
Home. Safe.

"Là, ci darem la mano
Là mi dirai di si
Vedi, non è lontano
Partiam, ben mio, da qui.
Partiam, ben mio, da qui."

He is almost touching her hand.

Maria. Answer : *"Vorrei."*

MARIA

"E non vorrei."

LUCIO

"Vorrei".

Maria hesitates.

MARIA

"E non vorrei."

A soft yell offstage.

Beppino. Oh and the bread. This talking...

She moves towards the stairway.
Pauses.

When I come back, and for ever after, we will
pretend you never said what you just said.

LUCIO

I spoke. No, I sang, to your heart. And you heard me.

MARIA

The words were never said.

She goes up stairs.

LUCIO

You heard me. The words are inside you now. The words are there. They exist.

There is a knock on side door.

They can't be cancelled. They can't be taken away. I lost my profession, my country, my job.

A knock.

They can't take away my words, my body.

A knock.

They can't take away my acts.

A knock.

I am here.

The side door opens. Candida enters.

CANDIDA

Permesso. Anyone home?

Louder.

Permesso... Oh, you are here. Why didn't you answer the door? I was standing there knocking and knocking. And the wind! I am blue, quite blue.

She starts unwrapping.

Such a chill. Walking over was bad enough. I was cold and felt so odd. And then knocking and knocking...Maria is here, isn't she?

Maria enters.

MARIA

Ciao, Candida. Let me take your coat.

LUCIO

Is Beppino upstairs?

MARIA

He's playing with his building blocks.

Lucio goes to the stairs and walks up.

CANDIDA

That man has potential. He is good looking enough.
There's a classy air about him.

MARIA

He is educated.

CANDIDA

Right. As I said. But his rudeness! He gets worse
everyday.

MARIA

If only you had known him at the beginning, when
I first arrived. No one could touch him for courtesy.

CANDIDA

Umm. Must be the air here. Or maybe the water.

MARIA

Are the men back?

CANDIDA

In full force. All over my kitchen: retelling their tales
of glory, plucking feathers, pulling out innards.
Bleech. I can't stand the smell. It's too much for me.
I can't even stand the thought of it. I left immediate-
ly.

MARIA

They are fixing supper?

CANDIDA

Can you believe it? Mario, he is so sweet, told me to
insist you come too.

MARIA

I don't know. I should stay here.

The phone rings.

CANDIDA

It's just as well I don't have to cook. I think I'm coming down with something.

MARIA

Again?

Staring at the phone.

CANDIDA

Again. There's no end to it. None. It's no wonder I get depressed. Aren't *you*?

MARIA

Coffee?

CANDIDA

I thought you would never ask. Aren't you going to answer the phone?

MARIA

It won't be for me. Who would call me?

CANDIDA

Maria, it could be important.

MARIA

Her hand on the phone.

Always, I can't understand.

She lifts the receiver slowly.

Allo?

Silence.

No.

Pause.

No.

She stares at the receiver and then at Candida.

Hung up.

CANDIDA

Who was it?

MARIA

Who knows. I couldn't understand one word.

CANDIDA

Probably a wrong number.

MARIA

I hate that phone.

CANDIDA

Reminds you of the world out there. No, I don't blame you. Just today, walking over, it was so cold. The streets so ugly. As I was saying — twice, twice, everything spun around me. Maria, will you be a dear and let me have some of this broth. It would do me good. And I can never stand to make it. The smell...

MARIA

Lucio didn't drink his coffee.

CANDIDA

Typical. I said he was getting ruder every day.

MARIA

He has been eating very little lately.

CANDIDA

God-forsaken place. Okay, I am joking about the air and water but this is still the frontier. We can't expect refinement.

MARIA

She is distracted.

No. Not refinement.

CANDIDA

All our men, yes I am including our husbands. Oh thanks. Did you put some extra salt in? You never use enough salt. All of the men spent too long in those work camps up north. They didn't see women for months. Wait, what am I saying, even when they did get to Edmonton they saw women — oh, is there any parmesan — but they were not really in contact with any respectable women for years. Oh dear, it is impossible to get any decent cheese here. When I get home I am going to eat and eat: cheese and salami and ice cream and tomatoes that taste like tomatoes. I don't care if I gain weight. When I remember how picky I used to be. Mother would have to beg me to eat. I didn't know how good everything was.

MARIA

Maybe that is what growing up means.

She stares into the bread bowl but does not knead.

CANDIDA

By the time we arrived, they had completely forgotten how a man should act around a lady.

MARIA

What?

She pokes dough.

CANDIDA

Are you paying attention, Maria? You are in a daze today. I was just saying the time in the work camps ruined the men's manners. Nico thinks it is fine to blow his nose with his fingers, to burp or fart and then to smile as if he had done something wonderful. And don't tell me it is just him. They are all alike. Well, maybe not in front of you...

24

Maria takes the bowl to the garbage and dumps the contents.

CANDIDA
Maria! What on earth?

MARIA
It did not rise properly.

CANDIDA
Couldn't you re-knead it or something? We all look forward to your bread. Isn't it usually baking by now? Nico will be so disappointed.

MARIA
It has never happened before. Not like this.

CANDIDA
Well, never mind. Not your day. You forgot to give me any coffee, you know.

MARIA
I must have made a mistake.

CANDIDA
It happens to the best of us. As I keep saying to Nico: a slip, fine, but we have to try and maintain some standards.

MARIA
There was too much cold air.

CANDIDA
Did Cesare ever tell you about the cock measuring contest they had? These two guys, Nico never would tell me who, were boasting and boasting about their size and prowess.

MARIA
I should have put the heat up.

CANDIDA

Then one of the others suggested they put their money where their mouth was, or their meat.

She giggles.

Or whatever.

MARIA

Fresh bread.

She speaks very quietly to herself.

You take back his look, you snatch the bread from his hand.

CANDIDA

So Mario, trust him, puts this metal ruler down on the radiator. Everyone was ready. You can imagine. Anyway you know how thick his callouses are. He casually holds it up against the first idiot who volunteers.

MARIA

Senza pane tutti diventano orfani. (Without bread, everyone is an orphan.)

CANDIDA

He screeched bloody murder, of course. Animals, all of them.

MARIA

Had enough?

She clears the table.

CANDIDA

Suddenly she becomes serious.

I never imagined, growing up, what men were really like. I thought it was all flowers and sweet melodies.

MARIA

If only we had listened.

CANDIDA

Pardon me?

MARIA

To the older women, to the proverbs. My step-mother used to say: "When a girl is born, a servant is born; when a boy is born, a lord."

CANDIDA

I suppose. I just wanted to get away: from the village, from the life my mother and my sisters lived, and, especially, from those older women who were always watching... and judging.

MARIA

If we had listened, we would have known.

CANDIDA

So? If we'd known, if we would have been warned, we would have accepted it all easier? I don't think so. Not me.

MARIA

You do believe in some of what we were taught as children.

CANDIDA

Brainwashing.

MARIA

Standards? Manners? You said...

CANDIDA

I had to leave. I had no choice. A woman has to marry.

MARIA

Some of the old beliefs? I am not sure myself. Superstitions or...

CANDIDA

And if there is even a hint she has been...emotional, human, unlucky, no one wants her. That's your old beliefs for you. No one wants her.

MARIA

No, not that, I meant practical advice.

She stares into the sink.

CANDIDA

I had to leave. But I did not escape.

MARIA

About nursing babies or ...the evil eye, for example. I was 14 when I left home to work as a maid.

CANDIDA

I can't stand another winter. My health is not up to it. Or my nerves.

MARIA

So I knew before I met Cesare what it was to be an immigrant, to live in a cold city, among strangers. I knew. Winter comes. It cannot be stopped.

CANDIDA

I told you about my dizzy spells. Those pains in my belly. I keep going back to Dr. Ciaro. I need him to tell Nico I have to be sent home. For my health. Not back to the village, of course. I thought of renting a little apartment in Rome.

Maria keeps returning to the sink. She makes washing gestures. She lifts the basin, takes a few steps, and then returns it to its original spot.

CANDIDA

Florence might be nice. Maria, are you listening to me? What now?

MARIA

Nothing. I am just trying to remember something.

CANDIDA

Like what to do with dirty water?

MARIA

It's nothing. Please. You were saying, the doctor says there is nothing wrong with you?

CANDIDA

He just keeps asking questions, lots and lots of questions. About Nico and me. About when we — you know. You would blush. You would.

MARIA

You're joking.

CANDIDA

I am not. "And then what does he do? And then?" Last time, he did an exam. I was lying there, legs spread, and he put his hand on my thigh, and as he talked he started to inch upward. "You need a release," he says. "All your problems will be over," he says. *Uno sfogo.*

MARIA

You better find yourself another doctor.

CANDIDA

"The organism needs an outlet." Oh, Maria, you should see your face. You are still the little village girl; old beliefs, practical advice. Different times, a different place.

MARIA

Perhaps you are the one who is still the country girl. Be prudent. Some things never change. And you are a married woman.

CANDIDA
Santa Maria, piena di grazia.

> *The front door-bell rings.*

MARIA
Candida, come with me. It may be someone selling something and you understand more than I do.

CANDIDA
I should never have told you any of it. How could a woman like you understand?

> *The door-bell rings again.*

MARIA
Please, Candida.

> *Maria goes to the door and begins to open it. Candida stands up and moves towards the door.*

CANDIDA
I never considered giving in; it is just the idea, the possibility...

MARIA
Vorrei e non vorrei.

CANDIDA
What?

MARIA
Come on.

> *A postman is at the door. He holds out a letter.*

POSTMAN
Registered letter for Mr. Legato. Sign here.

> *Maria stares at him and then turns to Candida.*

CANDIDA

Sign the form. The form he is holding. Really Maria, don't tell me no one has ever gotten a registered letter before.

Maria signs. Candida moves back to the main room.

CANDIDA

To herself.

Be prudent. Easy for you Maria. What temptation have you ever had to deal with? Let's face it; some women have what it takes and some don't. Poor, poor Maria.

Maria closes the door and stands at the bottom of the stairs, staring down at the letter.

MARIA

Thank you, Candida. I did think that he expected me to sign. I wasn't sure. I never am.

CANDIDA

You are too afraid of making a mistake. What would it matter? Hey, Miss, oops, Mrs. Prudent, Mrs. Cautious, Mrs. Afraid-of-her-own-Shadow?

MARIA

I know. I know. Cesare always says... It's just... I have to take the letter up. It's from Milvia — finally. Lucio has been waiting and waiting. Let's hope...

She goes up a couple of stairs, then stops.

Candida, you and Nico, you can learn together. You can teach him how to touch you. Cesare and I were such innocents, such, such innocents; still, we found the way.

31

Maria goes up the stairs. She pauses and then knocks at Lucio's door. Candida makes a face and then begins to mimic a school lesson. Lucio opens his door.

MARIA

A letter. For you.

Lucio takes the letter and holds it out, staring at the envelope. Maria begins to turn away.

LUCIO

So, at last it has come. The " Dear Lucio letter."

MARIA

You can't be sure.

LUCIO

I can. I have been warned. By my dear old friends, by my concerned family.

He slowly tears open the envelope.

I used to live for letters. Don't go. You should hear all her evasions and excuses.

MARIA

She waited a long time.

LUCIO

She betrayed me.

MARIA

But... you...

LUCIO

Yes, you — and I.

MARIA

No, I meant.

LUCIO

Who stopped waiting first? She or me? Eh, Maria?
Registered, special delivery. All finished now.

He begins to rip the letter.
Maria is edging away from him.

She or me?

He drops the bits of letter.

An official stamp. One hundred measly lire.

Lights out.

SCENE III

Evening.
Lights up on the main room. Group in
action. Riccardo and Mario are playing
cards. Candida is setting up the record
player. Maria distributes glasses and then
wine.

MARIO

To Candida.

I see your husband's absence has not slowed you
down any.

CANDIDA

Why should it?

She glances at Maria.

Well, if he insists on getting stinking drunk and
passing out...

RICCARDO

Down girl. He was not drunk. Just tired.

MARIA

You said Nico had been working overtime all week.

CANDIDA

So, I should sit at home, patient Griselda, and watch him breathe in and out?

MARIA

No. No. It is good to have you here. The baby cried for hours after you left this afternoon. I was feeling a bit desperate.

MARIO

We all need company, friends. I asked Lucio to come and join us, but he wouldn't.

MARIA

I finally realised I didn't have any milk. Luckily I had some formula and a bottle stored away.

RICCARDO

It was the same this morning. He wouldn't come hunting. Would have done him good to get out.

CANDIDA

Odd, you mean you just dried up — like that?

MARIO

Not him, he has to sit and brood in his room.

MARIA

I don't know. Oh, I'll probably be fine tomorrow.

RICCARDO

He has always thought he was better than us. How many times has he reminded us that he graduated from high school or that he was a policeman or that he had a few poems published or...

MARIO

Porca miseria, will you play?

CANDIDA

Have a beer. Isn't that supposed to help?

RICCARDO

He probably has enough salted away to last awhile.
He has always been tightfisted.

MARIO

I know this is hard for you, fleabrain, but try to talk
and play at the same time.

MARIA

In the village they used to say if a man...

> *Candida's expression is skeptical. Maria*
> *shakes her head and does not finish what*
> *she was going to say.*

RICCARDO

To Maria.

He is not sticking you for the rent, is he?

MARIA

What? Oh, he wouldn't.

RICCARDO

He is not the first to lose a job. We all have. But he is
the first to stop trying, to give up and hide away.

MARIA

Maybe it seems a bit useless. He has been working
and saving for this future with Milvia and then she
suddenly marries someone else.

CANDIDA

You're kidding. When was this?

MARIA

Her letter came today but I think he knew already.

MARIO

Word is that she was…is pregnant.

CANDIDA

Poor kid.

MARIA

Where did you hear that? Not from Lucio…

MARIO

I have an aunt in Castelfranco.

RICCARDO

He probably doesn't even know.

CANDIDA

I wonder if knowing she was, would it make it worse or better?

RICCARDO

He is well rid of her.

MARIO

They say: "Women and cows from your home town."

MARIA

What are you saying? She was from his town. They were still in school when they started going together.

MARIO

What can you expect? All those years of waiting. He opened the road for others. Oh, excuse me, Maria. It is true. That is why I am going to do it the way Cesare did. Fast. Go home, choose, and tie the knot. Bang, bang, bang.

RICCARDO

It is different with a woman like Valentina, a woman
you can trust. You should see how she writes to me.
Such words.

Lucio enters while Riccardo speaks.

LUCIO

With disgust.

Pretty phrases. The words mean nothing.

RICCARDO

How do you know? Not everyone's alike.

LUCIO

Oh? The words are all alike. " I think of you always"
— doesn't she? Though she couldn't possibly. She is
a busy girl, works in a hotel, if I remember correctly.
Probably spares you a moment once a day. When
she wonders when you are going to make your
America.

RICCARDO

You're mistaken.

LUCIO

" How I long for you", she writes. Ah I am not that
mistaken. Why should she long for you? What is
unique about you? She is surrounded by men all day
— bell-hops, waiters, managers — even the cus-
tomers, real men, right there around her, not an idea
on the horizon.

MARIA

Enough, Lucio.

LUCIO

Right. " I will never get enough of my Riccardo,"
she writes. " I pray each day for your safe and quick
return." Though it is the money she is praying for.

37

RICCARDO
How dare you!

LUCIO
Oh don't take it so personally. It is the same for all of us. Look at poor old Mario. All those pretty phrases in that letter from his mother. She misses you, she misses you, but she was the one who pushed you to come here — for the family.

MARIO
My mother...

LUCIO
Your mother, your family, all our families, even our damned homeland, chose us as sacrifices to their contentment, their well-being. Need money? Ship off a son. A mistake? Ship off a daughter.

MARIA
Why don't you sit down?

LUCIO
We work and work. Machines.

RICCARDO
I have not seen you working much lately.

LUCIO

He remains standing as he talks.

To send back dollars. And their letters — oh, they say they love us, but the dollars are what they really love. " Still, no work?" " We are sad to hear." Sad, sure, because the money flow has been cut. " Sad, sorry, sympathetic... blah, blah." The words are nothing. Formulas. They do not know what it is to live here.

He takes a big bite of a sandwich.

MARIO

We are working not just for them but for our futures, for our childrens' futures.

LUCIO

The future. What future? You think we will be able to go back and take up where we left off. Haa...! Did anyone from your village ever emigrate and then return?

MARIO

Well, there were a few...

LUCIO

Sure, many left, but only a few made it back. And in what state?

RICCARDO

What are you getting at?

LUCIO

Happy? Healthy? The same as they left? Or were they bent and twisted from work and struggle?

RICCARDO

It is different now. We are raising some capital so that...

LUCIO

To Mario.

L'Americano fesso. The American blockhead. Don't you remember? No gratitude, no love.

He speaks to all.

One of my neighbours went to New York so his brothers could be educated, so his sisters could marry well. When he returned, he was too ignorant...

In Candida's ear.

39

...too vulgar for those he had raised up with his own sweat.

MARIO

An odd case.

LUCIO

Is it?

CANDIDA

It will be different for us.

LUCIO

Why will you not remember? The returned are ridiculed and mimicked.

MARIA

In my village we used to say: "You have forgotten how to speak."

CANDIDA

Don't you start. You speak Italian as well as you ever did.

LUCIO

L'Americano fesso.

RICCARDO

He remembers the past. It is different now.

LUCIO

We have lost. No place there. And, dammit, no place here.

He drops the remains of the sandwich.

Why do I bother talking to you lot. *Siete tutti fessi.* You're all blockheads.

He exits back upstairs.
The others are silent. Then Candida puts a fifties rock'n'roll song on the record player. She begins swaying to the music.

40

CANDIDA

Damn him. He has to put a damper on everything.

Mario drops his cards, stands and extends his hand to her. They begin to jive around the room.

RICCARDO

Ehi, malzcalzone. You desert me?

MARIO

He sings a couple of words of the song.

I cannot resist a beautiful woman.

RICCARDO

Be careful or Nico will be resisting *you.*

Mario's hands stray a bit.

CANDIDA

Hey...

RICCARDO

When the cat's away...

MARIO

Who are you calling a mouse?

RICCARDO

Who has fur and a wiggly nose?

CANDIDA

What?

RICCARDO

Fur and a wiggly nose.

MARIA

Minnie mouse. She just needs some felt ears.

RICCARDO

Exactly.

CANDIDA
" Doo waa didi.."

MARIO
" Dam didi do..."

Dramatic dip.

We soar. We fly.

He turns volume up.

CANDIDA
We are the greatest. Lets rock until we drop.

MARIO
Rock.

Maria turns down the volume. Candida and Mario groan.

MARIA
You will wake up the children.

RICCARDO
Youth.

MARIA
I have always loved to dance.

RICCARDO
I cannot picture you... dancing.

MARIA
Just cleaning and cooking? You would be surprised.

RICCARDO
I did not mean...I do remember you and Lucio a few times...years ago now. Was it the tango you were so good at?

MARIA
Tango, foxtrot, waltz.

RICCARDO

Natural talent.

MARIA

I did not come here straight from the village, you know. I used to live in Milan.

RICCARDO

Oh a big city girl.

MARIA

She laughs.

Not quite. But I am not what you all seem to think me either.

Cesare enters. Maria goes to him and helps him with his coat.

CESARE

What is all the racket about?

RICCARDO

The master of the house has come.

MARIO

I had forgotten what he looked like.

CESARE

Turn that thing down.

Mario dances over to the record player and advances the needle.

MARIO

A slow one.

RICCARDO

Latin-lover. If only he knew how to dance.

CESARE

Supper?

MARIA
Almost done. Wine?

CESARE
You have to ask?

CANDIDA
Cesare, you missed quite the meal at my house.

MARIO
Four geese.

CANDIDA
Pasta, wine.

MARIO
Lots and lots of wine. Nico opened his cellars.

MARIA
I didn't go.

Maria pours out wine for all.

CESARE
You should have. No need to stay locked up here day after day.

RICCARDO
Very good, Cesare. Encourage her, now that there is no chance of her going.

CESARE
Unfair. I am always telling her she should go out. Even the doctor said. Maria, am I not always telling you?

Maria is staring at the dancers.

MARIA
I am sorry. The baby cried and cried..

CESARE

I bought that pram. She has hardly used it. Admit it, Maria. Maria.

MARIA

To the dancers.

You're out of step.

MARIO

Never.

Mario twirls Candida, then finishes off with a deep back bend.

CESARE

Where is Nico?

RICCARDO

At home. Asleep.

CESARE

When the cat...

MARIA

It has been said, Cesare, it has been said.

Mario sits back down at the card game. Candida turns off the record.

MARIO

Applause? No applause.

Beppino enters in his pyjamas.

BEPPINO

Daddy.

Beppino goes to his father. Cesare hugs his son and pulls him onto his knee.

CESARE

You know I haven't seen you for so long I think you have grown. Such a big, big boy.

Mario stares at the plate Maria is preparing. She carries it to Cesare.

MARIO

We should have saved you some of the goose.

CESARE

Not for me. No blood offerings.

RICCARDO

Hypocrite. You make a big deal about hunting and guns, but you eat as much meat as the rest of us.

MARIO

Staring at the cards.

Here we go. We might as well give up on this game.

CANDIDA

Losing, are you?

CESARE

There is a difference. I see a difference.

MARIO

We should start again. With some bets this time.

RICCARDO

Come on, Cesare. We expect more than that. What is it about you and guns? A phobia? Some sermon you have heard?

CESARE

What is it about you that can kill animals not from necessity but for sport? Not sure you are a man? Do you have to prove yourself with your metal phallus?

Maria steps in between.

MARIA

Stop. Both of you. Cesare, sit down, be quiet and eat. Riccardo, you sit too.

RICCARDO

He...

MARIO

Poker, that will keep our attention.

RICCARDO

Cesare likes to feel in charge. Imposing a few ar-bitrary rules gives him a sense of power.

Laughter.

MARIO

No guns in my house.

More laughter.

RICCARDO

Emperor of a miniature kingdom. The boss.

CESARE

Look, you...

MARIA

I said stop! May I remind all of you that there is a child in this room. Now, Cesare, eat your dinner.

> *She pours another glass of wine for Cesare. She puts the bottle away in the cupboard.*

The rest of you have had enough, more than enough. Don't make a face, Riccardo. You have been unfair. Cesare has always been against guns. Even in the army.

CESARE
Not easy to avoid them there. I did not even know
what the term "conscientious objector" meant. I
just refused to touch a gun.

RICCARDO
You are lucky that it was the Italian army. They
never have enough guns to go around. They were
probably secretly relieved. Oh, good. One extra.
Ah, Italia, Italia.

Everyone laughs.

CANDIDA
Laugh all you want. The thought of home... If I
could, I would kneel down this minute and kiss the
earth of my beloved homeland.

MARIO
Listen to her — "beloved homeland."

BEPPINO
Can you play with me now, Daddy?

RICCARDO
She is a southerner. She is doomed to excess.

CESARE
Italia. Mother and whore. She sells herself, no,
worse, she sells her children for cheap labour.

BEPPINO
Look at the house I built today.

RICCARDO
You've been listening to Lucio.

*He leans over, picks up a building
styrofoam block and tosses it at Cesare.*

Try the theatre.

CESARE

He catches the block and throws it back.

Cazzo.

Beppino, laughing, starts to toss the blocks about.

CANDIDA

She begins singing the Italian national anthem as she throws some blocks herself.

"Italia, sei bella."

MARIA

Be careful. *Dio buono.*

They gradually divide into two groups. Candida, Riccardo and, eventually, Maria are on one side of the room. All three of them are singing the anthem. Blocks are flying everywhere.

MARIO

We have to sing too.

CESARE

"Casetta in Canada" would be appropriate but...

CANDIDA

Ouch.

BEPPINO

Got her!

CESARE

We need something with more spirit.

RICCARDO

Bull's eye!

CESARE

"Bandiera rossa la trionferà."

Mario and Beppino begin singing with Cesare. The battle continues, both sides singing loudly, trying to drown out the other. There is much giggling.

CESARE

We are winning.

RICCARDO

Never. For the honor of our homeland, onward!

Lights out.

SCENE IV

Two weeks later.
The main room is empty. Lucio comes down the stairs and enters.

LUCIO

Maria...Maria.

MARIA

From offstage.

One moment.

She enters slowly, dressed in a bathrobe.

LUCIO

Where is Beppino? I thought he might like to go for a walk.

MARIA

He is with Candida. She took them both. My head. I couldn't.

LUCIO

You trust her, that *bamboluccia*? Not me. Not for a moment. I will go...

MARIA

Calm down. Beppino will be back soon.

She turns.

LUCIO

He grabs her by the wrist.

Wait, I have something important to tell you.

MARIA

My head. Later.

LUCIO

Listen. It has to be said now.

MARIA

Let go.

LUCIO

If you listen.

MARIA

Lowering herself into a chair.

As long it is not the Don Giovanni trick.

LUCIO

What are you saying? This is serious.

MARIA

Quickly then. Please.

LUCIO

I wrote a letter to Cesare. I stuck it in his lunchbox.

MARIA

A letter? About the rent? He has not spoken about it.

LUCIO

No. No. I had to allay his suspicions. For your sake.

MARIA

His suspicions? What on earth are you talking about?

LUCIO

I hate lying, but I did it out of my respect for you.

MARIA

What are you saying?

LUCIO

You want to keep up the charade.

MARIA

The charade?

LUCIO

Beppino. The fact that he is my child. My flesh. If Cesare stops running long enough to put two and two together, we will be discovered.

MARIA

We?

LUCIO

Yes, *we*. All that has been between us. Especially Beppino. If you just look at him, you can tell. It is time he knew. I know, you do not agree. So to forestall trouble — we all know how hot-tempered Cesare is — I wrote to him saying no matter how it seemed, Beppino was not my son.

MARIA

Lucio. How could you?

LUCIO

So you do not need to be angry with me anymore. You have been so cold. Now I have done what you wanted. Cesare is probably reading the letter this very moment. I wrote it so cleverly that he will be fooled. You can come to me again, when he is asleep. Like you used to. I would wake up and you would be there, standing by the bed, glowing in the dark. Your beauty...glowing...

MARIA

Rising.

Lucio, I never came to you. Never. There was never anything like that between us.

LUCIO

How can you lie so calmly? You think I do not remember those nights? Your touch.

MARIA

Clouds, all clouds.

Slowly.

We never loved one another. Beppino is not your son.

LUCIO

Puttana! You stand and stare into my eyes and lie and lie. You can go to the devil, you whore.

He starts to leave, stops.

Clouds? You are grounded in the filth of your mind.

He goes up the stairs. Yells down at her.

Whore.

Maria sits down again. She stares out at the audience. The phone begins to ring. She looks at it once but does not answer it. Riccardo rushes in from the outside and grabs it.

RICCARDO

Hung up.

He turns and sees Maria.

Oh, you are here. Why didn't you? Is something wrong? You are rather pale.

> *Maria does not answer. Instead, she goes up the stairs. Riccardo picks up what he has come back for. He is on his way out, in a rush. Candida and Beppino are at the door, trying to get in.*

CANDIDA

Ouch.

RICCARDO

We should run into each other more often.

CANDIDA

As long as I do all the running into. That hurt.

RICCARDO

Your poor little foot?

CANDIDA

Where is Maria?

RICCARDO

Upstairs. The phone was ringing and she didn't answer.

CANDIDA

Beppino, go find Mamma and tell her I am here.

> *Beppino goes upstairs.*

She has one of her headaches. That's why I had Beppino.

RICCARDO

It seemed more than that. She wasn't herself at all.

> *Maria appears on the stairs.*

Look, I've got to run. Back soon.

> *He leaves.*

CANDIDA

Too bad you are having such a tough time today —
head and all. I am having a wonderful day, perfectly
wonderful. My feet are no longer touching the
ground. Aren't you a teeny bit curious? No! Well, I
booked my flight home. First thing this morning.

Maria enters the main room slowly.

MARIA

You convinced Nico you needed a holiday.

*During the following dialogue Maria is
moving around the kitchen. She hesitantly
collects oil, salt and a pitcher of water.
She sets them on a tray. She seems to be
going through a mental check list.*

CANDIDA

I knew I would.

MARIA

When do you leave?

CANDIDA

January tenth. One day snow and beastly cold...
The next blue skies, nothing but blue skies.

MARIA

Be realistic. The skies will be blue here and grey
there.

CANDIDA

The sun will be shining in my heart.

She giggles.

I told you I was happy.

*She promenades, presents herself to an
imaginary passer-by.*

Spring comes early in the South. I will need new
clothes. No use buying anything here. They have no

idea of style. Can't you see me in a sky blue dress, white collar, a new haircut. On the *passeggiata*, the eyes of the young men. Oh, I haven't lost my looks yet.

MARIA
How long are you planning on staying?

CANDIDA
We will see.

MARIA
Nico has not set a deadline.

CANDIDA
I haven't told you all my news. I went to the doctor yesterday.

MARIA
He finally agreed to talk to Nico about your health?

CANDIDA
No. I don't need him to any more. Come on, congratulate me.

MARIA
You are expecting?

CANDIDA
Candidina, Mammina. He cannot possibly expect me to rush back. He knows how delicate I am. I need the support of my family.

MARIA
I was sure I would die when I had Beppino. I have never felt so alone.

CANDIDA
I am not having this baby surrounded by strangers.

MARIA

It was a nightmare. I was so frightened to start with; you know, my mother died in childbirth. They would not let Cesare stay. I couldn't understand the nurses or the doctor, except when he yelled, "Too much spaghetti", and pointed at my stomach.

CANDIDA

I am saving up all these stories to spring on Nico at the appropriate time. I have some gruesome ones about nervous breakdowns.

MARIA

So, how do you feel? Any morning sickness?

Maria dips her fingers in the oil, then touches it to the blankets in the cradle as if she were annointing the forehead and the lips of the baby. She shakes her head. Pauses.

CANDIDA

Actually I haven't felt this good in a while but I'm not going to let Nico know that. What are you doing?

MARIA

What I can.

CANDIDA

Pardon? Maria, you have not been your old self lately. Is there something you want to talk about?

MARIA

I have to protect my children.

CANDIDA

From what? They are both perfectly healthy.

Maria is mixing the salt and water.

MARIA
Malocchio. When I was a child.

She pauses.

Best be prudent, my aunt would say.

CANDIDA
Ah, the old ways. Don't waste your breath, Maria.
We have to look out for ourselves.

MARIA
I can't quite remember how it goes.

CANDIDA
After the birth, I will come up with another excuse.

MARIA
You are leaving Nico.

CANDIDA
Not really. He is free to join me. No, Maria, sit down.
Listen. We do not belong here on the edge of the
world. I have to go home. Not the village, of course,
Rome or Rimini. I do have to.

MARIA
Un bel dì. Cesare has promised me. Home. As soon
as we have enough money saved. Our house over-
looking the valley.

CANDIDA
Oh, sure. Nico makes promises too. But how long?
The years pass.

MARIA
Ed aspetto, aspetto.

> *Beppino runs in holding a large toy
> truck.*

MARIA

Careful of my things. That's good. Stand here a minute. You were a long time getting that toy.

BEPPINO

I was talking to Lucio. Playing in his room. Mamma, Lucio has this big gun.

CANDIDA

Gun! Cesare is going to have a fit.

Maria bends her head for a second. Then she begins the rites with Beppino. There is a sound at the door.

Back already.

She rises and goes to the mirror on the wall to check her reflection. She is applying lipstick when Riccardo and Mario enter.

RICCARDO

Both here?

MARIO

Finally, some real women.

CANDIDA

You don't say hello anymore? Such courtesy.

MARIO

Buon giorno. Good day, good day. " How are you, Maria?"

Maria barely nods. She is washing Beppino's arms.

RICCARDO

We brought donuts.

CANDIDA

Donuts? A bit perverse.

MARIO

Riccardo said your head was bad. I'll make some camomile, that might help.

> *Maria shakes her head. She constantly stops, gazes at Beppino and then starts again.*

CANDIDA

Donuts. Better watch yourselves. Next it will be popcorn.

MARIO

Peanut butter. Marshmallows.

RICCARDO

Ugh, not marshmallows, never marshmallows.

> *Beppino pulls away from Maria. He runs to Riccardo and gazes into the box of donuts.*

RICCARDO

Go ahead. Any one you want. That's right.

CANDIDA

Corrupter of the innocent.

> *She takes a donut.*

RICCARDO

Not me. The boy was born here; he was born with certain tastes.

MARIO

> *With a slight sneer.*

Canadian tastes.

MARIA

Beppino.

Beppino returns to his mother. As he takes a big bite, a piece of donut falls into the bowl. Maria lets out an exclamation.

RICCARDO

We were trying to sweet-talk the girl in the donut shop for so long — we had to buy all these.

MARIO

All day we have been trying.

CANDIDA

Not bad these. The same girl, all day?

RICCARDO

No, no. Different girls, same result.

CANDIDA

The great Latin-lovers- failures! Serves you right.

Everyone, except Maria, is eating donuts.

MARIO

We didn't expect much. We would have been happy with a pleasant conversation.

RICCARDO

It is odd. At first we did not know the language. I could understand our never connecting then. But now we know the words.

He poses.

" Girl, pretty, you walk with me."

MARIO

" Tits, ass, f—." Excuse me, Maria.

MARIA

Staring at the bowl.

Pardon?

RICCARDO

To Mario.

Don't worry. She simply does not understand.

To everyone.

Now we know the words. Yet, for us they do not seem to mean what they are supposed to mean. Pretty from our mouths is not the same as "pretty" from the mouth of Mr. Edmonton.

CANDIDA

Maybe you just don't have what it takes.

RICCARDO

I never had any trouble in Italy. Oh I could tell you stories. Swedish women, English, American even. No trouble, no trouble at all.

CANDIDA

Could it be your grammar?

MARIO

Grammar? Who gives a shit about grammar? We are not in school now. No, I've talked about it with Maria. Haven't I, Maria? Maybe it is our accents. Oh, I don't know.

RICCARDO

Maria, how *should* we talk to these Canadian women? Come on, give us some of your good advice.

Maria stares from one to the other.

MARIO

Maria, is it your head?

CANDIDA

What do you expect? With all your hot air.

RICCARDO
Speak to us, Maria.

MARIO
Speak.

CANDIDA
Lay off her.

RICCARDO
Speak, Maria.

MARIO
Say something, anything.

RICCARDO
Did we offend you?

MARIO
I shouldn't have said.

RICCARDO
It is just talk, Maria.

BEPPINO
Mamma.

Maria gets up, goes over to Beppino, touches his head, then exits, with the bowl of water.

MARIO
What's with her?

CANDIDA
She wasn't wearing her coat or boots.

RICCARDO
All that stuff she was doing?

CANDIDA
She has these weird ideas.

MARIO

I was going to make her some tea.

RICCARDO

She will catch her death of cold.

CANDIDA

She was not so bad. Not till you two came in. Idiots. You do have to go on and on.

MARIO

We didn't say anything we hadn't said before.

CANDIDA

Riccardo, run after her. Take this coat.

Sound at door. Then Riccardo and Maria collide at doorway.

MARIA

Without the words, I cannot... Cannot... I. Forgive me.

She exits up stairs.
Lights off.

SCENE V

Later that evening.
Lights on the empty stage. Sound at door.
Cesare enters. He puts his lunch box down
on the table. He seems tired. He looks
around, hesitates, and only then begins to
slowly take off his scarf and coat.

CESARE

I should have seen it coming; I should have taken note. If I were home more, if I weren't blinded by weariness.

He puts coat down, looks around for
wine, glass.

Unable to see, unable almost to move. Bone weary. Especially tonight.

He puts the bottle and glass by the
lunchbox. He rubs his arms.

The feel of coming winter, the premonition of old age.

He is obviously in pain.

It took me by surprise. Sitting there with my boss on my lunchbreak. By surprise. That's why I lost control. Hot tempered tears and words. In front of him. I exposed myself, became the cliché of the Wop. I can hear him now. "What can you expect from people like him?"

He opens his lunchbox and takes out a
crumpled letter.

What can you expect. Damned lies. Any man would lose control, any man. A veil of insinuations over the truth.

He smooths out the letter.

"Despite all that has happened Beppino is your child." How dare he? Inform me my son is my son. Suggest...suggest that my wife...

> *He crumples the letter and throws it into the corner.*

He can go to the devil. And stay there. I will not help him again. Never. After all these years, I thought we were friends, brothers, and all along he...
If I had him in my hands right now, I could... Maria. Where is that woman tonight? Maria! He deserves a good beating. Yes, Maria, he deserves it. Oh I can imagine what she would say. Calm yourself. Control.

> *Pause.*

She would be right.

> *Maria, in a dressing gown, is at the door watching him.*

CESARE

Maria — were you sleeping? Why didn't you come?

> *Maria enters.*

MARIA

Supper?

CESARE

Wine. That's all I want tonight.

> *He pours wine.*

MARIA

I told you this morning my head hurt.

CESARE

Ah, your head. Yes. I forgot. Your head.

Maria is slicing bread. He goes over and grabs her.

Have you lost it — this head of yours? Is that why it hurts more and more often these days?

MARIA
You got the letter.

CESARE
I got it, oh yes. I got the letter. In my lunchbox. You should have warned me. At least that.

MARIA
You don't believe what he said.

CESARE
You have read it already? Did you help him write it too?

MARIA
No...He told me today.

She picks up the letter, smooths it out and reads it.

CESARE
He has always had a weakness for you. I am not a fool. I have noticed. And you...

MARIA
And me what? What are you saying?

CESARE
Sometimes, in your eyes, when you look at him.

MARIA
You are both full of fantasies.

CESARE
I have left you alone a lot. I am guilty of that. And he is much easier on the eyes, and the ears, than I am.

MARIA

I never...

CESARE

Maria, I...

MARIA

He's sick, Cesare. Don't you see?

CESARE

I see that you have been alone, alone and far from home. I could understand... Tell me the truth. I must know.

MARIA

I thought you knew who I was and where I came from.

CESARE

It is not as if you loved me at the beginning. You said...

MARIA

God help me.

CESARE

I didn't mean...

MARIA

I said and I swore. Do you doubt me?

> *Maria returns to the letter, tears it into small pieces, throws the bits on the floor and then exits, all without a word. Meanwhile, Cesare becomes more conciliatory. He gets down on his hands and knees to pick up the bits.*

CESARE

I was trying to explain why he...

> *He follows Maria out.*

We have all gone mad.

Lights on Lucio, in his room, holding a gun.

LUCIO

Singing.

"*Io penso alla notte ed alla mia casetta*
Alla mia vecchietta che sempre aspetta
Mamma, morirò di nostalgia.
L'amore del paese e della Mamma
È un gran fiamma che bruscia mio cuore."
My heart burns, that's true enough. I am dying of nostalgia. Of all that has and has not been. Maria, Maria.

Mario, during the song has come out on the landing.

"*Terra straniera, quanta malinconia*
Quando ci salutiamo
Non so perchè
Tu mi gettasti un bacio."

MARIO

Porco Guida. It is one in the morning.

He knocks on Lucio's door.

Some of us need to sleep. Some of us have to work in the morning.

LUCIO

Still singing.

"*Fuggisti via*
E pure adesso
Te lo confesso
Non penso che a te."

Riccardo joins Mario on the landing.

69

RICCARDO
Quiet! For the love of God.

LUCIO
"*Mi sono dimencato
Dei tuoi capelli
E della bocca
Che era la mia vita.*"

> *Riccardo opens Lucio's door. Lucio aims
> his gun at him.*

RICCARDO
God! Put that bloody thing down.

MARIO
Is he serious?

> *Lucio closes his door with his foot. He
> opens the window, aims and shoots.
> Maria and Cesare, hearing the shot, run
> in. The others stand on the landing chat-
> tering.*

MARIA
Mimma... Bep... What?

MARIO
It's Lucio.

RICCARDO
His face.

CESARE
Come down, all of you, and let me talk to him.

> *Chatter.*

Come. I'll handle this alone.

> *The others reluctantly go downstairs.
> Cesare stands staring in silence at the
> door.*

Lucio, come out and talk to me. We have to speak...It is very difficult through the door... Please, open the door.

LUCIO

I don't have to do anything.

CESARE

Of course you don't. I am asking you to choose to put down that gun. To come out so we can try to talk.

He starts turning the door handle.

LUCIO

I will shoot. You will be blown to a thousand pieces.

CESARE

You've had a difficult time. I understand. We all do. You need to go home.

LUCIO

It is not the place. Not this particular place. Not the house. Not the walls. Not the closed door.

CESARE

For the sake of all the years we have been friends, Lucio, listen to me.

LUCIO

Friends? Is that what we have been? Or two men caught in the same place, in the same time.

Caressing his gun.

CESARE

Listen to me. I have told you more than once about how in the army I was anti-gun.

LUCIO

The myth of Cesare. The ever-repeating stories.

CESARE

Have I ever told you how it started? You must hear me. You must understand.

> *The two men can speak either at the same time or normally. However, their voices at some points, at least, should overlap as in an operatic duet.*

LUCIO

It's not the place. It's the way it is.

CESARE

I was sixteen when I joined the partisans, a boy.

LUCIO

Who can truly understand another?

CESARE

I was no hero. There was no real choice.

LUCIO

We are trapped.

CESARE

Either you were with the Germans or with the partisans. We lived by night.

LUCIO

Trapped by ourselves and by our visions.

CESARE

Work and trade, all in darkness.

LUCIO

Each one of us tries to impose our truth on the outside .

CESARE

The priest used to say mass at five in the morning, thinking that at least then the men could safely come out of hiding.

LUCIO
On the foreign land.

CESARE
But the Germans found out and emptied the church, carted the men off.

LUCIO
Vanity.

CESARE
I used to sleep each day in a different place to avoid being caught and taken off with the others to a work camp.

LUCIO
Vanity and delusion.

CESARE
When I joined the partisans, at least I wasn't just the hunted. I was doing something.

LUCIO
A futile struggle to impose our pitiful meanings, to impose our words.

CESARE
And there were companions.

LUCIO
When I first arrived I was so desperate to understand. I would listen so carefully, trying to pluck out the familiar, to pin down what was being said. Yet, as I learned English, I began to see that I still did not quite understand.

CESARE
I do not need to tell you what the SS did as the German army retreated.

LUCIO
No one knows.

CESARE
It's best not to talk too much of these things.

LUCIO
It is not just a question of different languages ...or different cultures that divide us.

CESARE
They are more than the heart can bear.

LUCIO
All language is foreign.

CESARE
Our rage then. We blew up bridges. They rebuilt them. We blew them up again.

LUCIO
A word for me is not the same word for her.

CESARE
They could not get across the rivers and their rage was boundless.

LUCIO
We are all in exile.

CESARE
They burned down my cousin's house thinking I was there.

LUCIO
Our minds play games with meaning.

CESARE
One of my uncles was one of the thirteen hung on the evergreens of Bassano.

LUCIO

Not the same. Too many words. And for what? Not one of us sees what the other sees.

CESARE

He yells.

Lucio!

Now he is trying to answer Lucio so the effect is no longer that of intertwining monologues.

You are right. I talk too much. It is one of my biggest flaws. That and my quickness. I am quick to anger. Then I was ruled by my anger, night and day. It was not just the group's anger. No, it was personal anger. I planned an ambush. Sixteen years old I was. Thirty retreating soldiers. I felt so jusitified, so clear. I did not hesitate. I rejoiced as the gun recoiled over and over...Afterwards, as soon as I looked...afterwards I knew, and how I knew, how wrong I had been.

LUCIO

Animals, all of them. The truth is in the flesh, in hunger and in lust. In rage. Everywhere, buried beneath the words, buried deep, deep in the eyes, I can spot it. I...

CESARE

Animals, but so was I, ruled by anger. Animals, but also boys my age. Not SS, but boys, trying to get home. Animals, all of us. I am trying to tell you, I agree. I swore there, standing over that blood, never again. Never. Lucio, please understand. We do not always know what we do. We do not have that control. Put that gun down. For your own sake. There is another way.

LUCIO

For you.

He yells.

For you.

CESARE

You need help.

LUCIO

Go away. Leave me alone. I am sick of you and your words. Sick. Smug bastard.

CESARE

I will not leave till...

Lucio aims his rifle at the window and shoots.

LUCIO

Now you listen. Next time it will be through the door. Or through you.

Lights out.

SCENE VI

Later that night.
Maria enters in her dressing gown; she wanders about the empty room.

MARIA

Oil, salt, oil...How can I sleep with this head. Oil. The pills don't help. One, two, three... I have lost count, but still no help. Oh.

She stares at a spot on the floor.

Who?

She takes out rag and attacks the floor on her hands and knees.

Wine. They could at least tell me. But oh no. It's up to me. All up to me. All the mess. The filth. Until that day. Until we go home.

She stands up and puts rag away.

I wanted to nurse both my babies. At home, with the help of my aunt and my sisters, I could have, I know I could have. But here, with Beppino... "You're too tense," the doctor said. Too tense. "Too alone," he should have said. Then, with Mimma, Lucio looked at me with his dark heart. Oil, salt and water.

She begins again to gather together the oil.

And there was no more milk. Poor mad Lucio. Now Candida is going too. Oil and salt, flame and water. Yes, fire was a part of it. But what part?

She stirs together salt and water.

At least she chose. Who will I talk to? The other boys will be going soon to marriage or home. There will be no one...Poor mad Lucio. No one in the long days. No one to keep back the cold as I wait and wait.

She picks up a baby blanket.

I will only have you. And Beppino and Cesare, of course, of course. Until we go home. Just us. Oil and salt, flame and water. You wash the child with the salt and water and then throw the water away — far from the house and in the form of a cross. If I could remember the words. It does not work without the words. We will go home, Mimma, we will go home to our house and our valley. *La ci darem la...* I will hold you and your brother so tightly, so safely till that day. I should have had you swaddled after you were born. Cesare laughed. There is safety in the old ways, safety. The old rites. Oil and salt, flame and water. If I could remember the words. I only heard them a few times as a child, mumbled over my head or that of my brothers and sisters. I left the valley before I had the age or the wisdom to learn from the older women. Each word must be exact. Oil and salt, flame and water —that I remember. The words, the words.

> *Lights out.*

SCENE VII

> *The next day.*
> *Riccardo and Mario enter, chatting, yet still noticeably nervous.*

MARIO
The pulley was a brilliant idea, brilliant, admit it.

RICCARDO
Not bad, though it took you long enough. And it was damn cold standing out there.

MARIO
Greetings all.

> *He goes up to Maria and puts an arm around her.*

Victory, Maria.

RICCARDO
We have been talking to the girls in the convent on 107th Street. Sending up notes, anyway.

MARIO

Getting back notes. That is the important part. You two are awfully glum.

RICCARDO

He points upwards.

He is still...?

CESARE

I listened at the door for a while but I could not hear anything.

MARIA

There have not been any sounds for awhile. No footsteps.

CESARE

He is probably asleep.

MARIA

Or dead.

CESARE

Don't be silly, Maria. We would have heard a shot. Or something. Look, why don't you go up and listen. You know I'm going deaf.

MARIA

No, I don't want to go up.

RICCARDO

It can't go on. We have to do something.

MARIO

It makes it hard to sleep at night, knowing he is in such a state.

RICCARDO

It is not safe for any of us.

CESARE

Especially not for him.

RICCARDO

What are you going to do, Cesare?

MARIO

You could start by cutting off his meals. Starve him out.

CESARE

Forget it. He'll get angrier. His rage ...

RICCARDO

You should call the police.

MARIO

Or the mental hospital.

CESARE

What good would that do? The state Lucio's in. Shit. We'd have a gunfight. Or he would just shoot himself. No, I won't have it.

RICCARDO

They are trained to handle this kind of thing. What do we know?

CESARE

We are his *paesani*. Surely we should be able to help him. Somehow.

MARIO

Look, you tried. Ric tried. Nico tried. He gets madder.

MARIA

You really think ... the police?

MARIO

No, I think Cesare's right. We do not need outsiders. We should handle it ourselves.

CESARE

How?

MARIO

We could grab him on his way to the can.

RICCARDO

He takes his gun with him. I saw him.

MARIO

Okay. We wait until he's asleep. We climb up to the outside balcony, quiet as cats,and burst in on him. Catching him unaware.

RICCARDO

It would make a good story.

MARIO

Exactly.

CESARE

Carrying guns?

MARIO

Of course. No reason to be stupid.

CESARE

Stupid? Your whole idea, that is what is stupid.

MARIO

You haven't come up with anything. You just want us to wait, all of us jumpy.

RICCARDO

All of us in danger.

MARIO

What are we waiting for? For him to blow his brains out?

RICCARDO

If he doesn't get one of us first.

CESARE
We owe it to him.

RICCARDO
Doesn't he owe it to *us*?

MARIO
Maybe we could drug his food. Get something to knock him out.

MARIA
He barely eats a thing. If he did decide to eat, if we put in too much, it could kill him.

CESARE
He's in trouble. At least, we owe him thoughts before actions.

RICCARDO
Maria hasn't tried to talk to him.

MARIA
I don't know.

RICCARDO
You were friends. He thought the world of you. If he listens to anyone, he will listen to you.

MARIO
He's right. Lucio always respected you.

CESARE
Why are you speaking of him in the past tense?

RICCARDO
Come on. It can't hurt.

MARIA
It won't do any good. There is nothing I could say.

CESARE
It might help.

MARIA

It won't. But I will try. Just to show you.

*Cesare has already risen. Maria motions
him to sit.*

MARIA

I will go alone.

*She mounts the stairs . She pauses outside
Lucio's door and then knocks.*

Lucio, it's Maria. Please open the door.

LUCIO

Vaffanculo.

MARIA

I can't talk to you through the door. Please.

LUCIO

I do not want to be talked to. I am sick of all the
useless sounds you have all been making. None of
you are strong enough to face the truth. I know how
alone I am, how alone each one of us is. Alone
without escape.

Those first days here, my search through alien
streets for a trace of the familiar, that was reality. At
home, it was easier to be fooled, to be taken in by
the farcical comedy of family life. We cling to our
illusions. We lie even to ourselves. But go out to the
country and stand beneath this western sky. You
will feel it.

MARIA

Please, Lucio. You need help. You are not yourself.

LUCIO

I am truly myself.

MARIA

No matter what you believe. No matter how hard it is, you have to go on. You must not do this to yourself.

LUCIO

It is you who is not yourself. You have denied me over and over.

MARIA

There was never anything between us.

LUCIO

Nothing between us. Never. We are all separate. And the comforts of true flesh? The links of desire? Itches? Frenzied ticks. Friction.

MARIA

For the sake of your mother, Lucio, you have to see a doctor. If she had known of this, it would have hurt her so much.

LUCIO

My mother's dead. And soon... soon... I will be dead too.

MARIA

Non dico più niente.

> *She starts to leave. Lucio bounds to the door, unlocks it quietly, then shoves it open, gun still in hand. He stares at her down the rifle butt. She stares back and then turns and goes down the stairs.*

I just made him angrier.

RICCARDO

Crazy with anger.

CESARE

Or despair.

RICCARDO
We have to call the police. It can't go on....The longer we wait the worse it gets.

Beppino calls out from the other room.

MARIA
Poor boy. He is not sleeping well. He senses something is up.

MARIO
He asked me yesterday why you would not let him go up and play with Lucio.

CESARE
That's it.

MARIA
What?

CESARE
Lucio has a special feeling for the boy.

MARIA
A feeling based on a delusion.

CESARE
Still... Beppino's the one.

MARIA
No.

CESARE
He is the only one who can go in, talk to him, get the gun.

MARIA
He is five years old.

RICCARDO

Now you have gone mad too. Bad enough to risk our lives. Now you want to put your only son, a baby, in jeopardy.

MARIA

You don't know what you are asking.

CESARE

Lucio would never hurt him.

MARIA

I don't like it.

CESARE

He is closed to us. We are all mixed up in his failure. Witnesses if nothing else.

MARIA

Call the police.

CESARE

We owe him another try.

MARIA

We owe him nothing, not after all these months.

CESARE

Maria, I cannot believe you are speaking like this. You have always been the kindest of women. And Lucio.

MARIA

At a certain point, you have to say: "No, enough, no more."

CESARE

We have to try to solve things quietly among ourselves. I learned very young. Guns and uniforms don't work.

MARIA

I learned things when I was young too. You have to think of your family and what you owe them first.

RICCARDO

Well put. She is right, as always.

MARIO

Listen to your wife, Cesare.

CESARE

Go to hell, all of you. Out of here. Idiots. I talk to my wife alone.

He chases the two men out. Beppino cries out again.

MARIA

Now you've woken him.

CESARE

Let me just bring him in here for a minute.

He goes to get Beppino.

MARIA

My life.

She moves about restlessly.

Blessed Virgin Mary, help me.

Cesare re-enters with the boy.

CESARE

Bad dreams.

MARIA

Come to Mamma.

To Cesare.

I am not letting go of him.

CESARE

Maria, I understand how you feel.

MARIA

Do you? Do you really know? I doubt it.

CESARE

You are afraid. You think I'm not? Fear and anger, we must fight them: for Lucio and for us.

MARIA

I will keep him safe.

CESARE

When you had Beppino, when you were wheeled into that delivery room, you felt absolutely alone.

MARIA

I have said it many times. Alone. Until I felt Beppino in my arms.

CESARE

That man upstairs can see no escape from his solitude. He thinks we are all animals, owing only to ourselves and our desires. We must show him...

MARIA

Show him? He won't see.

CESARE

Not now. Eventually. He will. Maria, you had no right to accuse me of not thinking of my family. And before the others. When even now, I am thinking of us.

MARIA

How? Tell me how you are thinking of Beppino.

CESARE

You know I work day and night for you, the house, for our America. Either Lucio's right and there are no bonds, or I am.

MARIA
And, as always, you are so sure you are right.

CESARE
No, not sure. Sometimes I see the same world he does. We must pretend. There is community. There are responsibilities. At least pretend. Otherwise, Beppino and Mimma will only inherit curses. You saw the war. Chaos and misery. Why else did we all have to leave?

BEPPINO
Mamma, you're hurting me.

CESARE
Son, you know Lucio loves you.

BEPPINO
I love Lucio.

CESARE
And he would never hurt you.

BEPPINO
I know.

CESARE
But Lucio is not well.

BEPPINO
He has a cough.

MARIA
No, Beppino, he is confused. He is angry.

CESARE
He won't put down his gun. But if he doesn't...

MARIA
He could hurt himself.

CESARE

He won't listen to us.

MARIA

But he loves you.

CESARE

You must go to him, talk to him.

MARIA

Oh, Cesare.

CESARE

A chance.

MARIA

Move slowly. If he does anything odd, if his face changes, if he moves quickly, run, run out of the room.

CESARE

To Maria.

Steady. Choice and chance.

BEPPINO

I'm scared.

MARIA

We are all afraid. You are the only one who can help Lucio.

CESARE

You want to help him?

Beppino nods.

MARIA

I will be at the bottom of the stairs.

CESARE

You do agree? You want to help him?

Beppino nods.

MARIA

I agree.

CESARE

Beppino, you must listen one more time.

They bend over Beppino, talking in low voices. They walk him, slowly, to the stairs. They stand and wait as he walks up. A light remains on Beppino and softer lights on Maria and Cesare's faces.

BEPPINO

Outside Lucio's door.

It's me, Lucio. Open the door.

LUCIO

Go away, Beppino. Please, go away.

BEPPINO

I won't. Not until I see you. I won't go away.

Lucio is torn but finally, slowly, opens the door. Beppino lays his hands on the rifle and gently takes it from him. When he has put it aside, he and Lucio embrace. The light on Lucio and Beppino darkens; they continue to embrace through the following epilogue. Cesare and Maria face and address the audience.

CESARE

I phoned the hospital. It seemed the right thing to do. He needed help and he was now disarmed. "Come in a plain car," I said, " with no white uniforms, no restraining jackets. Let him feel he has chosen." " Yes," they said, "yes." But they came with their barred van, with their uniforms and their jackets.

MARIA

When he saw them, he tried to run out the back door. A man was there, ready. You have denied me again. He said to me: " Again."

CESARE

We visited him every Sunday.

MARIA

Though at first he refused to see us.

CESARE

As soon as he seemed better, we signed the release forms.

MARIA

He still was not quite who he had been.

CESARE

We thought he needed to go home.

MARIA

We paid for his ticket, wishing we could go oursel-ves.

CESARE

Mario was going to be married so he took him and left him in the hands of his brother and sisters.

MARIA

Three years later, it was our turn to go home.

CESARE

We stayed a year.

MARIA

It didn't work: for the children who saw Canada as home or for Cesare who had changed. Lucio was right. We no longer fit our place.

CESARE

We wanted to see Lucio before we returned to Edmonton.

MARIA

They told us, he had gotten another gun.

CESARE

They let him die.

MARIA

After all that, they let him die.

Lights out.

The End.

Printed by
the workers of
Ateliers Graphiques Marc Veilleux Inc.
Cap-Saint-Ignace, Qué.